An Exercise in Happiness

The Ultimate Kids Guide to Happiness

By Patrick McMillan

Published by: Kids Can Do Anything, LLC

An Exercise in Happiness—The Ultimate Kids Guide to Happiness

1st Edition, 2010

Author: Patrick John McMillan

Printed in the United States of America

ISBN # 978-0-9845299-0-2

This Book Belongs to:

Heidi Nicole Heckard

Name

School _MMES_

Teacher _Ms. Seelk_   Grade _1_

Table of Contents

Happiness Exercises

This book was written for my sons,
Hayden and Liam.
I am so grateful and honored to be their dad.

Welcome to the Kids Can Do Anything program.

—— Kids really CAN do anything! ——

Most kids want to be happy. They want to reach their goals. They also want to feel great about themselves and others.

Are you a kid who wants to be happy? Then ask yourself three questions:

Is being happy important to me?

Is reaching my goals important to me?

Is feeling great about myself and others important to me?

In the *Kids Can Do Anything* program, you will learn that being happy is easier than you think. You will learn that reaching your goals is easier than you think. You will learn that you can feel great about yourself and others.

The lessons you will learn in this program are real. They are called "Lessons in Happiness." These lessons will teach you a new way of thinking. You will learn to use the power in your mind. You will learn how to be a *happier you*.

You will also complete exercises so you can practice this new way of thinking. These exercises are called "Happiness Exercises". They will help you make the lessons you learn, become a part of your life.

It's time to discover three things that can change your life. Can you guess what they are? They are your:

Thoughts   Feelings   Actions

You are the only one who thinks your thoughts. You are the only one who feels your feelings. You are the only one who does your actions. No one else thinks, feels, or does these things for you. Not your mom or dad, your brother or sister, or even your friends. There is only one of you in the world and you are the only one able to live your life!

There isn't a computer in your brain that tells you what to do. No other person can tell you what kind of a life you will have. When you learn the Lessons in Happiness and practice the Happiness Exercises you will have the power to change your life!

Don't think these powerful lessons are just for kids. These lessons and exercises have been around for hundreds of years. Until now, these lessons were taught only to grownups. But kids can learn these powerful lessons too. Kids can do anything!

These lessons and exercises will be a fun adventure. They will give you rewards that will last a lifetime. I am so excited for you!

Patrick McMillan
An Exercise in Happiness

The World's Most Powerful Words

Grateful Words

There are a few words that give you a wonderful feeling when you use them. Every language has these words. They are grateful words.

Sometimes you have feelings that aren't so wonderful. There are two words which make those kinds of feelings go away and bring you joy and happiness. These two words are:

Thank you has the power to change the world. If you want to change the world, try using these two words. You will bring a wonderful change into your life.

True Feelings

Have you ever been grateful for something? Have you ever felt like saying *thank you*? Did it make you feel unhappy? Probably not. That's because being grateful is an easy and powerful way to create happiness.

Have you ever heard anyone say *thank you* but you weren't sure they really felt grateful? Did you ever say *thank you* to someone but didn't feel truly grateful? Sometimes we say words without truly feeling what we say.

We all have a special gift. We are able to sense feelings. It is easy to spot when someone feels grateful. You know the feeling of being grateful. The more powerful your grateful thoughts are the more you will find yourself feeling happy!

me of the top scientists in the world studied these feelings. They discovered that people, who actice feeling grateful every day, make their lives better. The scientists found that grateful people e longer, get sick less often, and have more friends. They even do better at school! People who are ly thankful, are happier.

Exercise in Happiness will help you understand the amazing power of being grateful. When you mplete the Happiness Exercises, you will understand what I mean. It is important to do these ercises with feeling.

> Some people have to "see it to believe it."
> However, the truth is you must
> **believe it, so you can see it**.

eeling grateful has amazing effects which you can really see. It's as easy as writing a list! I do this ersonally and it is very effective.

ry Writing a List

ave you ever felt that a friend is bothering you? Have you ever felt frustrated at your mom, dad, ister, or brother? When you start to feel bothered or frustrated at someone, try writing a list.

s quickly as you can, get a pencil and a piece of paper. Find a quiet place to sit. Then make a list! Vrite down all the reasons you are grateful that person is in your life. You will find that you only have o write down one or two things on your list, and your frustration will drift away.

Sometimes people don't feel happy, but I became a happier person when I remembered to be grateful every day. I am grateful for all the people in my life, including me!

Little Things

Try to be grateful every day. When you wake up in the morning you can start being grateful. You can be grateful for the comfortable bed that you slept in, the water you use to brush your teeth, and the house you live in. You can be thankful for your family and friends, and your teachers at school.

You can be grateful for the little things you don't think about very often, but you would miss if they were gone. Some of these things might include the sun, the rain, the trees, and the animals. How about cars, trains, and buses? What about really little things like shoelaces, buttons, and pasta?

When you feel thankful for these things, you feel happier. When you feel thankful, you are able to make the world a happier place.

Showing Appreciation

Remember the first two words? You can make the world happier by saying those words out loud. When you say "thank you" the person you thanked will usually say:

you're welcome!

When the person you thanked says "you're welcome", you know they appreciate your thanks. Are *thank you* and *you're welcome* just words? Yes. But when you say them with feeling, the power they have is gigantic.

They make the person who says them feel great! They create a wonderful *feeling* to those who *hear* them. Then, the person who says "thank you" and the person who says "you're welcome" become happier people.

aking Things Better

e next three words are powerful. When you say
em with feeling, they make you and the person who
ars them feel wonderful. Hopefully, you will not
ed to say these words very often. Everyone must
y them sometimes.

ometimes we say or do things that cause
happiness to ourselves or others. When you take
sponsibility for what you have done or said, you
come a powerful person. When you say these
ree words and really feel them in your heart, the
orld becomes a happier place. Can you guess these
ree words? They are:

I am sorry!

howing Kindness

he next three words have a special power. When a person hears them, he or she feels better.
aying these words is very important. Saying these words shows the world what kind of person you
re. Saying them shows others you are strong and kind. It shows them you understand how others
eel. It shows them you care about people too.

I Forgive you!

The words in this Lesson can change the world!

Why am I Here?

People Are Special

Can you imagine the world without the people you know and love in it? The world just wouldn't be the same without them. These people are special. Every person has the power to change the world. This includes you!

It doesn't matter what you look like, or the color of your skin, hair, or eyes. It doesn't matter how tall or short you are. It doesn't matter how big your house is or how many toys you have. What matters is the "you" inside. This is the you that thinks thoughts, feels feelings, and does actions.

The Lessons in Happiness and the Happiness Exercises will help you discover the you inside. The you inside loves to learn new things. This you is able to imagine and to make believe. This you is able to solve problems. When you tap into the power of the you inside, you can live your dreams.

> You are the creator of your thoughts,
> your feelings, and your actions.
> Therefore, you are the creator of your whole life.

Imagine if Walt Disney was never born. Imagine if Martin Luther King Jr. or Abraham Lincoln were never born. Our world would certainly be a different place.

You might think to yourself *"I could never be the kind of person Walt Disney was"*, *"I could never become the President"*, or *"I could never become a famous inventor of anything."* But remember, you are the creator of your whole life. What you think, feel, and do can change the world. **The world is a better place because you are here and you can do anything!**

3 Thoughts Create Everything

Almost everything you use in your daily life was once a thought in someone's mind. Before something becomes a thing, it is a thought. Thoughts really do become things. Some of those things are toothbrushes, cars, video games, and computers. Some of those things are pajamas, ice cream, pizza, and umbrellas. You probably can think of more important or fun things you use each day.

Your thoughts create how you feel, who you are, and what you do. But who or what creates your thoughts? You do!

Science has discovered that you have thousands of thoughts each day. Wow! You have so many thoughts you cannot pay attention to them all.

Some thoughts create feelings. You should pay attention to the thoughts that create feelings. If someone says something to you, you might have a thought about what they said. The thought will create a feeling. The feeling might be happy or sad. The feeling might be loving or mad.

You may act a certain way because you feel a certain way. For example, your mom may make your favorite food for dinner. You may hug your mom because you feel happy.

Hot and Cool Thoughts

Many times we have feelings but we don't think about them first. These feelings just seem to happen! For example, if someone says something mean to you, you may have a thought which makes you feel hurt or angry. When you have those thoughts and feelings, you might want to say something mean, too. If you can't control those thoughts and feelings, they can make you feel hot inside. That is why we call them **HOT THOUGHTS**.

If someone says something mean, you can do something different. You can ask yourself, *"Is what that person said to me really true?"* Or, *"Is he saying it to see if he can make me sad or angry?"*

When you think about what happened and ask yourself those questions, you can change your feelings! Those kinds of thoughts and questions are called COOL THOUGHTS.

Most people care about you, but sometimes people might try to hurt your feelings. It's very important to remember, all they can do is try. Remember, only you can control your thoughts and feelings. Only you can change them! You have a special power to say, *"I control my thoughts. I control my feelings. No one else can make me feel angry or sad."*

Sometimes, you will have feelings you don't want. They come from thoughts that you are thinking. But you can think of something funny instead. Then, you can change your feelings!

Just the way a light switch turns on a light, you can turn on happy feelings. Just try telling yourself a funny joke or remembering a happy day, like your birthday. You may even make yourself laugh! When you laugh, you are feeling great and thinking COOL THOUGHTS.

Remember, if you think **HOT THOUGHTS**, you can change them. You can do that by thinking COOL THOUGHTS.

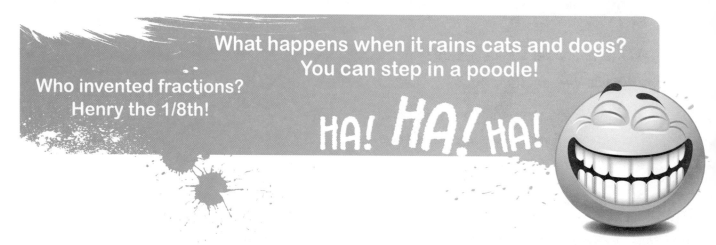

What happens when it rains cats and dogs?
You can step in a poodle!

Who invented fractions?
Henry the 1/8th!

HA! HA! HA!

every **HOT THOUGHT** there is a matching **COOL THOUGHT**. For example, you might think, *"I'm stupid"* but you can change that thought to a **COOL THOUGHT** by asking a question, *"Am I really stupid?"* Think of all the incredible things you have learned in school and at home. Think of all the amazing things you have done. Then you will see the answer is NO!

You might think, *"Everyone hates me."* You can change this **HOT THOUGHT** by asking yourself a question, *"Does everyone really hate me?"* You can probably name many people who really like or love you. Try to name them all. Then you will change that **HOT THOUGHT** to a **COOL THOUGHT**.

If you have **HOT THOUGHTS** about yourself or anyone else, they will not change, unless you change them.

Sad not Bad

Sad feelings are not bad feelings. This is important to understand. We all feel sad sometimes, but it is not bad to feel sad. If you are feeling sad about something, it's important to understand what is making you sad. Try asking questions to help you understand:

1. Is it something someone said to me that is making me feel sad?

2. Is it because I am unhappy about something I said or did?

3. Is it because something I tried to do, but didn't succeed?

If you answered **yes** to any of the questions this might be the cause of your sad feelings.

Now, try using some **COOL THOUGHTS** to answer those questions and change your feelings:

1. Was what the person said, true?
    Probably not!

2. Did I say or do something by mistake?
    That's okay. Everyone makes mistakes! Next time, I will remember what happened and try saying or doing something different.

3. Did I fail at something I tried to do?
    That's okay. Next time I will do better.

Get in the Habit

By now you know that your thoughts can change your feelings. By asking questions and answering them in your mind, you can feel happier. If you want to *feel* happy, you should think happy thoughts. The more you practice, the easier it becomes. Soon you will get in the habit of doing this. A habit forms when you think the same thought over and over again. A habit can form when you feel the same feeling over and over again. A habit can form when you do the same action over and over again. Soon, you don't have to think about your habit, it just happens!

Sometimes we have habits we *don't* want. At first, it may seem difficult to change an unwanted habit. But you have the power to make that change. You can *choose* to replace an unwanted habit with a habit that causes you to feel great. Soon you will see that the new habit has taken over. You can get into the habit of replacing hot thoughts with cool thoughts. Why not try it? It gets easier the more you practice doing it.

Remember:

1. Pay attention to what you want, instead of what you don't want.

2. Pay attention to what you can do, instead of what you cannot do. You will find you can do more than you think.

3. Pay attention to doing the best you can!

Your Feeling Magnet

When you think COOL THOUGHTS, the feelings and actions you want, will follow. Soon, you will be feeling the way you want to feel most of the time. It takes time and practice to learn how to think this way. Try it for one day and see what happens. By the end of the day, it should be easier. If you control your thoughts that create feelings for a week, it will be even easier.

Don't give up. It could take a whole month for a big change to happen.

When you have happy feelings, people notice it! The things you want to happen, will seem to happen! It's your thoughts and feelings which are making this happen.

This is called your Feeling Magnet. Your feelings attract people and things into your life, just like a magnet! Take control of your thoughts and feelings. Then you can choose to attract the things you want to attract. Soon your Feeling Magnet will attract more good things and happy feelings into your life!

Feeling thankful is a feeling that turns on your attracting magnet. When you are feeling grateful you become like a magnet. Like a magnet, you begin to attract good things into your life. These things will make you feel even more grateful. When you feel grateful often, your life will change.

Remember, what you think and how you feel can change your life. So think happy thoughts and you will have a happier life.

> When you are feeling grateful you become like a magnet. Like a magnet, you begin to attract good things into your life.

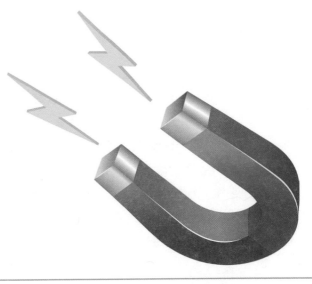

5 Choices

Vanilla or Chocolate?

What would you choose—vanilla or chocolate ice cream? Maybe you would choose strawberry, bubble-gum, or coconut ice cream.

Take a look at what you are wearing. What clothes did you choose to wear today? What color top did you choose? Think about what you ate for breakfast. Did you choose your own cereal? Did you choose what to have for lunch?

Some choices are very important. Who did you choose to play with at recess? Who did you choose to sit next to at lunch? What did you choose to tell your mom and dad about what you learned in school today? Did you ever choose to *not* tell your mom or dad something?

Your choices matter. Everything you will do depends on the choices you make. The kind of person you become, your grades at school, the friendships you make, and the sports or activities you participate in, will depend on the choices you make.

There is something else you need to know about your choices. You must know that your choices will affect others. You might choose to say or do something which causes someone else to have unhappy thoughts and feelings. What do you think will happen? Most likely, you will have unhappy thoughts and feelings, too.

You cannot control all your thoughts. Remember, there are thousands and thousands of them each day! But you can control some of them. When you have an important choice to make, pay attention to your thoughts. Think about what will happen *after* you choose what to say or do. Will it be the kind of choice your parents and teachers will think is right for you? Will you have reason to feel happy about your choice? Will your choice make others feel happy? If the answer is yes to all these questions, it is probably the right choice!

What Do You Think?

Your mind holds more memory than all the computers in the world. In fact, everything you ever learned, felt, or did, is still there! Many memories get hidden deep in your mind and you almost never think about them.

Sometimes, these memories seem to float to the top of your mind! For example, if you hear a certain song or smell a certain smell, an almost-forgotten memory might float up!

All your thoughts, even the hidden ones, will lead you to make choices. They will lead you to live your life a certain way.

Let me tell you about Napoleon Hill. He lived from 1883 to 1970. That was a long time ago. He sold millions of books about success in life. I want you to know some of his ideas because they can help you live your life. I have chosen three important ideas from Napoleon Hill's books.

1. Thinking something over and over again can help you reach your goals.

2. If you help others reach their goals, you will reach your own goals even quicker!

3. Every time you don't succeed, think about what happened. If you look carefully, you might find an important lesson.

Remember to choose your thoughts carefully. If you tell yourself you are able to do something, you really may be able to do it! But if you tell yourself you can't do something, you really won't be able to do it.

Thinking and Feeling Happy

Being Thankful

Remember in Lesson One we learned about feeling thankful? Feeling thankful can make you happier. Have you ever been thankful and unhappy at the same time? Probably not.

When you are thankful for something or someone, you get a great feeling inside. You also feel happy when you know that someone else is thankful for something you have done.

Reaching Goals

Have you ever worked hard on something and reached your goal? Were you proud of yourself for working so hard and being successful? I bet it gives you a happy feeling even now when you think about it.

Usually people feel happy when they work hard and reach a goal. When we try something and do not succeed, we can still feel great about ourselves for trying. Trying is important too.

Helping other people achieve their goals can make you feel happy. Most people reach some of their goals, but not all of them. Pay attention to how happy you feel when you reach your goals. Pay attention to how you feel when you try, but do not reach your goals. Remember, you can still feel great about yourself for trying.

earning

earning and trying new things can give you happy
elings.

you remember the day you rode your bike without
ining wheels for the first time? You will likely remember
at day forever.

metimes, when you are trying something new, you
ght need to get help from others. When they show you
w to do it, you will be able to teach others and help
em learn too.

Playing

One of the best things you can do to help yourself feel
happy is play! A lot! The kind of playing that can really
make you happy is the kind that uses your imagination.
Pretend and make-believe are incredible because they
can give you a wonderful feeling.

Imagine yourself as a superhero, the President, an
inventor, or a teacher! Being a great person, even just
in your imagination, will give you a wonderful feeling.

Imagine Your Life

Do you want to begin creating your happy life? Start by thinking happy thoughts. Imagine the rest of your life. Imagine what will happen tomorrow and the next day.

Imagining is like dreaming when you are awake. Your mind doesn't know that what you're imagining is just make-believe. It thinks your thoughts are real!

Imagine or dream about what will happen. You get to choose what you want to think about. It's as if you are creating a movie. Call the movie, "My Life." In your movie you get to make up the story. You also get to be the star!

Remember to Think Big! Think about all the awesome things you will do. Think about all the great people you will meet. Will you get a good grade on a test? Will you have a good friendship? Will you grow up and be someone who will change the world?

Your Think Big Board

An exciting activity to help you imagine what you want is to create a **Think Big Board**. Ask your mom or dad for some magazines. Tell your mom or dad that you want to cut some pictures out of magazines. Ask them for permission.

Look for pictures of people you would like to meet or be like. Maybe you would like to meet or be like a successful athlete or a famous world leader.

Next, look for places you would like to go. Maybe you would like to go to

y. Maybe you would like to climb a certain mountain. Maybe you want to go to an exciting city!

ally, look for pictures of things you would like to do. Would you like to fly on the space shuttle? uld you like to sail around the world or become doctor and save people's lives?

t out the pictures you chose. Paste them on a piece of poster board. Hang your Think Big Board in ur room where you can see it all the time. It can help you imagine the life you want!

Imagine. Imagine. Imagine!

ur Mind Movie

ask you to close your eyes and think about your bike, you do not see the words "my bike." Instead, u see a picture of your bike in your mind. This is because you think in pictures. If you think about ing something, like riding your bike, you will see yourself in a **mind movie**. It is like your eyes are e movie cameras. You are able to see a mind movie about something even if it is something you ve never tried before. Making a "mind movie" is also called being able to "visualize."

emember, your mind can't tell if something is real or just your imagination. It feels like it is real. It is most like you are really doing what you see in your mind movie!

verything ever made began as something someone visualized. Then, it became real. There is so uch power in imagining what you want in your life. Walt Disney first visualized what he wanted create. Everything he visualized turned out bigger than he ever thought it would. This is true for veryone who has ever accomplished their dreams.

ou have an incredible imagination, so have n with it. As often as you can, take the time to st sit and use your imagination.

What are Your Goals?

Do you want to accomplish something? Then set a goal! When you set a goal you are telling yourself, *"I can achieve something I really want to achieve."* You can set a goal to *be* something, to *do* something, or to *have* something.

A goal can be something new you want to learn. For example, I want to learn to ski, I want to learn how to play tennis, or I'm going to learn how to play guitar. You can set a goal to do well on your math test or to get along better with your brother or sister. You can set a goal to have more fun playing with friends or to be happy more often.

People set goals all the time. Some people set goals such as eating healthier foods and exercising more often. Some people set a goal to do something kind for someone every day. People set goals to become a doctor, firefighter, or teacher.

Sometimes people don't achieve the goals they set for themselves, and that's okay. Each time you set a goal and don't succeed, you have an opportunity. These opportunities will help you learn something new.

Whether you succeed or not, you should feel proud of yourself. You set a goal and tried to achieve it.

There are four main reasons people either don't set goals for themselves, or they fail to achieve them

1. They are not sure of what they really want, or they feel they don't deserve it.

2. They forget to write down their goals.

3. They don't take the ACTION needed to achieve them.

4. They don't see mistakes or failures as chances to learn something new.

t's look at each one of the reasons:

1. **They are not sure of what they really want to do, or they feel they don't deserve it.**

any people don't set goals because they're scared they may not reach their goals. We all deserve to happy, so set a goal to be happier.

n't forget, helping someone else be happy will make you feel happy! But remember, you deserve to happy, too.

you want to achieve your goals? Then remember to be sure of what you really want, and realize u deserve it!

2. **They forget to write down their goals.**

cientists have studied people who write down their goals. What they learned was that people who rite down their goals often achieve them! In fact, they are twice as likely to achieve their goals as eople who don't write them down.

ust writing down your goals makes your chances of achieving them much better. So don't forget to rite down your goals.

3. They don't take the ACTION needed to achieve them.

Now you know what you want to achieve. And you remembered to write it down. What comes next? ACTION!

Let's use our imagination to learn more about ACTION. Let's set a goal for today. How about having great time playing with your friends at recess? Sounds good! Write down your goal.

Now, can you think of an ACTION you might take to achieve your goal?

I can think of some ACTIONS that might help. You might try *being* a certain way. You might try being friendly, being fair, and being forgiving if someone makes a mistake. You might try being kind by inviting a "new kid" to play with you. These are all ACTIONS which might help you achieve your goal. These are just some ideas; there are other ACTIONS you could choose.

Remember, after you think of your goal, write it down. Write down at least one ACTION you will take to achieve your goal. If you think of more actions, go ahead and write them down too.

4. They don't see mistakes or failures as chances to learn something new.

There are big differences between people who achieve their goals and those who do not. The biggest difference is that people who end up achieving their goals, learn from their mistakes. Learning from your mistakes and failures is so important that it deserves its own lesson.

Mistakes Are Not Failures
& Failures are Not Mistakes

The first thing to know about mistakes is that everyone makes them! Mistakes are very important. They have to happen for you to learn. Every person makes mistakes and experiences failure. It's interesting that the people who are the most successful have made many, many mistakes. They have experienced much failure.

If successful people made so many mistakes, then why did they succeed? Because they knew an important secret to success: When you make a mistake or fail, you have a great opportunity! You have the opportunity to learn and do better the next time.

No one can be naturally perfect at everything. Sure, some people are very skilled and talented. But even the person who is the very best at *something* is not the best at *everything*. Therefore, when you try something new, you must know that it's okay to make mistakes. It's what you do with the mistake that counts.

Are you a person who tries something and gives up if you don't succeed the first or second time? Or, are you the type of person who can learn from mistakes and keep trying harder?

It's okay when things don't work out exactly the way you wanted. Your real power lies in your **BELIEF** in yourself. When you believe in yourself, you know that you can succeed in almost anything you choose to accomplish. You must always remember that mistakes are hidden opportunities.

Getting Up Again

When you fall down you get up again. That's the way it can be when you make a mistake or fail. Get right back up again! See where you can do better. The biggest mistake you can make is giving up.

Below are some important things to remember when you make mistakes:

1. Tell yourself *"I did the best I could with the skills I had at the time."*

2. Understand that everyone makes mistakes.

3. Make a list of the things you learned from the experience.

4. Remember that it takes lots of practice and usually quite a few mistakes to get really good at something.

5. Make a new plan, and use what you have learned from your mistakes.

A WISE, OLD TALE

A YOUNG MAN ASKED THE WISE, OLD MAN,
"HOW DID YOU GET TO BE SO WISE?"

"BY MAKING WISE CHOICES." THE OLD, WISE MAN ANSWERED.

"HOW DID YOU KNOW THEY WERE WISE CHOICES?"
THE YOUNG MAN ASKED.

"WHY, BY EXPERIENCE, OF COURSE." HE REPLIED.

"HOW DID YOU GET EXPERIENCE?" THE YOUNG MAN ASKED.

"BY MAKING POOR CHOICES!" SAID THE WISE, OLD MAN.

Taking Action

Let's try using your imagination in an amazing way. Imagine you are a bicycle. Think about what color you would be. Think about what you would look like. Imagine you are an awesome bike with great tires. Imagine that you can go as fast as you want.

You have places you want to go. These places are the goals you have set for yourself. All you have to do is go in the right direction!

You are able to go in the right direction, because you believe that you can get there. After all, you have handlebars. These help you steer. That way you can be sure that you are headed in the right direction. If you did not have handlebars, you would never be able to reach your goal. Handlebars are like the belief you have in yourself! If you do not believe you can reach your goals, you will not reach them. It's that simple.

Now, the only thing left to do is get those wheels rolling. You need to take *action*. You have to get going by stepping on your pedals. Not taking action is like taking your feet off your pedals. If you don't pedal, you don't move.

After you think about what you want to accomplish, choose your goal. Then choose what you need to do, to reach your goal. What next? You have to take action! The very first time you take action is like putting your foot on the pedals. Taking the first *action* toward your goal is one of the most important steps you can take towards reaching your goal.

Pay attention to each action you take. Each one is important. You will enjoy taking action even if you don't succeed! Seeing the hard work you put into reaching your goal will give you a wonderful feeling. You will learn more about yourself and what you are able to accomplish.

Imagine yourself, as you would like to be, doing what you want to do,
and each day, take one step…
—Author Unknown

Great People Speak

"All our dreams can come true, if we have the courage to pursue them."

—*Walt Disney, Artist and Inventor, 1901 - 1966*

"The child must know that she is a miracle, that since the beginning of the world there hasn't been, and until the end of the world there will not be, another child like her."

—*Pablo Casals, Famous Cellist, 1876 - 1973*

"Things may come to those who wait, but only the things left behind by those who didn't wait."

—*Abraham Lincoln, 16th President of the United States , 1809 –1865*

"I'm not afraid of storms; I'm learning to sail m own ship."

—*Louisa May Alcott, Author of Little Women 1832 –1888*

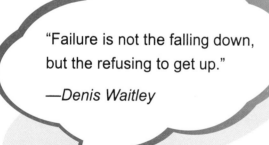

"Failure is not the falling down, but the refusing to get up."

—*Denis Waitley*

"A journey of a thousand miles begins with a single step." —*Chinese Saying*

"Nothing great was ever achieved without enthusiasm."

—*Ralph Waldo Emerson, American Poet 1803 –1882*

"If you dream it, you can do it. Always remember that this whole thing started with a dream and a mouse."

—*Walt Disney, 1901 - 1966*

"It doesn't matter how slowly you go – as long as you don't stop."

—*Confucius, Chinese Teacher 551 B.C.E. - 479 B.C.E.*

"Fall seven times, stand up eight."

—*Japanese Saying*

"All that I can, I will." —*French Saying*

"No one knows what he can do until he tries."

—*Publilius Syrus, Latin Writer, 1811 - 1896*

"Today is the day you make your choices for tomorrow."

—*Author Unknown*

An Inspiring Story

The picture above has a great story attached to it. This is a fifth grade class picture from 1975. It was taken at the St. Francis Xavier School in Burlington, Ontario, Canada.

I am the dashing young man in the white shirt and long hair standing beside the teacher. However, there is one student you might recognize. He is in the top row, third person from the left. Do you know who he is? That student is who this story is about.

name is Jim Carrey! You probably know him from his movie roles. He has played the Riddler
[o]ne of the Batman movies. He played Count Olaf in *"Lemony Snicket's, A Series of Unfortunate [Ev]ents."* He also acted in *"The Grinch Who Stole Christmas"* and *"Ace Ventura: Pet Detective."* Jim [i]s also the voice of Horton, in the Dr. Seuss story *"Horton Hears a Who."* Jim's story is an example [of] what An Exercise in Happiness can provide for you.

[Jim] had a passion for making people laugh. He practiced all the time and became very good at it. [Wit]h this passion, Jim also set goals which helped him become the famous actor he is today.

[Ju]st like you and me, Jim also had difficult times. He made mistakes, had failures and rejections, as [he] was trying to become an actor. When he started his career, he was booed off stage, and many [tim]es he auditioned for a movie part but he was rejected.

[Jim] told stories of how he would visualize being a famous Hollywood actor.

[He] wanted to reach his goals of becoming an actor just like you and I want to reach our goals. Jim [stu]ck to his goals through times when many people would have given up. Jim's story is an example [of] how the Lessons in Happiness and the Exercises in Happiness work.

[As] you can see in the picture, we look like a typical elementary school class. We didn't have the [coo]l clothes and stuff you have today, but we were pretty much like you. We wanted to be happy [an]d we wanted to make our moms and dads happy. We wanted to do well in school. We wanted to [ha]ve friends. We wanted to get along with our brothers and sisters. We even had some of the same [ch]allenges you have today!

[Th]e one thing we did not have was the *Kids Can Do Anything* program. This program gives us the [to]ols we need, to have the life we want.

[If] you read the lessons carefully, you will notice an important idea. That important idea is that being [ha]ppy is not something that just happens! We must work at achieving our goals. Then, we will be [h]appier.

[W]e all have times when we feel unhappy thoughts. We all have times when we make mistakes or fail. [B]ut even our mistakes and failures, can help us lead a happier life.

Remember—When you feel happy, you do better at the things you try to do.

Happiness Exercises: Instructions

Many great teachers have said that a *habit* is created when we repeat the same action every day. The Happiness Exercises are the *taking action* part of An Exercise in Happiness which will help you develop a "habit of happiness."

It takes time and practice to become really good at anything. The exercises in this workbook are your tools to learn how to control your thoughts, feelings, and actions. Remember, these tools have been proven to help people live happier lives.

My Commitment to Me

This is your first step in the Happiness Exercises. It's your written commitment to complete the Happiness Exercises.

My Amazing Me List and Amazing Me Word List

This can grow to be a huge list! The bigger the better! This is a list of the fantastic qualities which make you a great person. The list will include things you are capable of doing and being.

This list will also include things you will become capable of doing. All you need to do is focus and practice. Just making the list will give you a great feeling because you will start to see the wonderful person you are, and the amazing things you can do.

My Thought Shift List

This is a fun activity! Create a new list anytime you need to put your feelings back on track. Get in the habit of making this list and your thoughts will create a feeling of happiness.

The list should include things which make you happy. The list may include memories of when you did something. It may include places you want to go. It might include times you were proud of yourself.

My THINK BIG List

In this section, you will make a list of the wonderful things you want to be and do in your life. List the great things you would like to do, the amazing person you want to be, and the incredible places you would love to go.

See yourself in the future. Picture how happy you are doing these wonderful things, and having these great experiences. You can also create a "THINK BIG" board to go along with your list.

Wow! That Went Well

This exercise is done every Friday. Write a few sentences about something that went well during the past week.

This can be about anything. Write about how much fun you had with a friend, or about doing well on a test. Write about anything that went the way you wanted it to.

Try to notice which strengths you used from your *Amazing Me* list or the Amazing Me Word List.

My Thank You Letter

This exercise will give you such an incredible feeling of happiness! Write a *Thank You* letter to someone to whom you are thankful.

This letter can be given to whomever you choose. For example, are you thankful for your parents, your brother, your friend, or your cousin? Tell them why you are thankful and you will feel great.

When you see how happy this makes them feel, you will want to write another thank you letter. Write as many as you want!

THE DAILY EXERCISES

My Feelings Meter

The daily exercises will help you put all the lessons you have learned into ACTION. These exercis
work best when done in the morning. They can be done at home or in class. Your Feeling Meter
shows how you feel right now!

-3	**-1**	**+1**	**+3**
very upset or angry	upset. bummed out	I'm happy	I'm very happy

If you circle a -3, it might mean you are feeling very unhappy. You may have had a very rough start
to your day. You may be thinking HOT thoughts. You can use your Thought Shift List to help you
figure out how to feel better and create some COOL thoughts.

Go find someone who can help you feel better like your mom, dad, teacher, or friend. Turn to the
Though Shift List page and read about what makes you happy. Add to the list and if you don't have
room on the page, get another piece of paper. When you shift your thoughts you will start to feel a
feeling to match that thought.

Circling a +3 means you started your day off feeling great! You are in a great mood. You are very
happy and ready to have a fantastic day. You are in a great position to help a friend or family memb
feel better if their FEELING Meter is low.

Here are examples of the Feeling Meter:

+3 = "I'm feeling very happy right now, things are great!"

+2 = "I feel happy, things are fine."

+1 = "I'm okay."

 0 = "I'm not so happy, but not really sad either."

-1 = "I'm feeling a bit upset, maybe even a little hurt or sad."

-2 = "I'm quite upset right now."

-3 = "I'm feeling very sad/angry/scared right now."

atement of Gratitude

e quickest and easiest way to put you in a happy
od is to be thankful for something or someone.
member how great you felt when you wrote a
nk you letter? We all have so much to be grateful
 and if you write a gratitude statement every day,
u start to create a habit.

y Goal For Today

ese goals are what you want to achieve today,
morrow, next week, or next month. Look at your
nazing Me List to find things you are good at doing
being. Set your goals by using this list. Achieving goals
n give you a great feeling!

your goal is too easy, you will not get a very meaningful
eling. Set meaningful goals which require your attention
d focus in order to achieve them. Don't make your goals
o hard or you will feel frustrated trying to achieve them.

ly Action Affirmation

ne action affirmation statement is where you tell yourself
at you are capable of achieving your goal because you
now what action to take, to make it
appen.

ow that you have *An Exercise in*
Happiness, and you know how it works, you
ave a choice. Will you make a commitment to
ourself to have a happy life? Or, will you
ist let your life happen to you?

On the next page, is your opportunity to
nake a commitment to yourself.

ou know you can have the life you want
vhen you commit to doing what it takes to make
t happen.

My Commitment to Me

I, _____, am committed to completing the Exercise in Happiness program. I know when I feel great about myself and others, I am a happier person.

I promise myself that I will take a few minutes each morning and recognize my feelings, why I am feeling them, and to make a commitment to feeling the way I want to feel.

I also promise that I will write down something I am thankful for, my goal for the day, and my action affirmation.

I will begin my daily exercises on _____/_____/_____

I also acknowledge that I am special and
I can help others to see that they are special too.

Signed _____

Date _____/_____/_____

My "Amazing Me" List

This is a list of things you know you are good at doing and ways you are good at being. For example, *"I am a good student and I am very good at math"*, *"I am good at being quiet while my teacher is talking"*, and *"I am good at being on time for class."*

You will use this list to help me set meaningful and realistic goals for yourself. On the next page, there is a list of words you can use to describe yourself.

1_____

2._____

3._____

4._____

5._____

6._____

7._____

8._____

9._____

10._____

11._____

12._____

13._____

14._____

15._____

Amazing Me Word List

happy   helpful   courageous   confident   smart
wise   eager   strong   motivated   friendly
imaginative   fun   helpful   grateful   caring   sharing
loving   creative   fair   encouraging   motivating
daring   funny   honest   respectful   curious
love to learn   hopeful   forgiving   playful

On the lines below, write a list of the top five amazing words
which describe your strengths. Live each day using at least one of these
top five strengths you already have.

1._____

2._____

3._____

4._____

5._____

My "Thought Shift" List

On this page make a list of things which make you very happy!
For example, *"I love to listen to music"*, *"I like spending the night at my friend's house"*, or *"I love my puppy."*

The list can include memories, family, friends, pets, music, nature, and especially things you have accomplished.
These are COOL happy thoughts.

notice your feelings as you write!

My THINK BIG List

Make a list of what you want to be, and things you want to do, in your life. The items on this list should make you excited! For example, *"I would like to climb the tallest mountain"*, *"I want to be a veterinarian",* and *"I want to travel to another country."*

You can use this list to help you make your own THINK BIG Board. Don't forget to include things you will accomplish.

_____

_____

_____

_____

_____

_____

_____

_____

_____

_____

_____

_____

That Went Well

Write a few sentences about something that went well during the past week. For example, *"I learned to do a cartwheel with only one hand"* or *"I hit a home run during my baseball game!"*

Make your list on Fridays. Remembering things that went well will remind you that *you* made it.

First Friday

Date: _____

_____

_____

_____

_____

_____

Second Friday

Date: _____

_____

_____

_____

_____

_____

Third Friday   Date: _____

_____

_____

_____

_____

_____

Fourth Friday   Date: _____

_____

_____

_____

_____

Fifth Friday   Date: _____

_____

_____

_____

_____

If you recognize when things go the way you wanted, you will start to see how it is you that creates your life!

My Thank You Letter

Write a Thank You Letter to someone in your life. This exercise will give you a great feeling and you will likely want that feeling again. Write as many letters as you wish.

Person I wrote my Thank You letter to:

_____

I read or gave my Thank You Letter to them on: _____/_____/____

How did this exercise make you feel?

_____

_____

_____

_____

How did this exercise make the other person feel?

_____

_____

_____

_____

Daily Exercises in Happiness

I begin each day by noticing how I am feeling by looking at **My Feelings Meter**. I can either make it better or keep feeling great.

Then, I will write **My Gratitude Statement** because when I am thankful, I am happy! The next statement is **My Goal for Today**, which is what I want to accomplish. Finally, I will write my **Action Affirmation**, which is why I can achieve my goal, and what ACTION I will take.

Below is a list of statement starters to help you get started:

Gratitude Statement Starters

"I am so happy and thankful that…"

"I am lucky to be…"

"It's great that I have…"

My Goal for Today Statement Starters

"I am committed to being…today"

"I am working toward becoming…"

"My goal for today is to accomplish…"

My Action Affirmation Starters

"I will achieve my goal for today because I will…."

"I am capable of achieving my goal because I…."

"I can accomplish my goal because I …"

Day 1

My Feeling Meter Reading: -3   -2   -1   0   +1   +2   +3

(Circle your answer)

I can move my meter reading higher, or keep it up by:

_____

_____

_____

_____

My Gratitude Statement:

_____

_____

_____

_____

My Goal for Today:

_____

_____

_____

_____

My Action Affirmation:

_____

_____

_____

_____

Day 2

My Feeling Meter Reading: -3   -2   -1   0   +1   +2   +3

(Circle your answer)

I can move my meter reading higher, or keep it up by:

_____

_____

_____

_____

My Gratitude Statement:

_____

_____

_____

_____

My Goal for Today:

_____

_____

_____

_____

My Action Affirmation:

_____

_____

_____

_____

Day 3

My Feeling Meter Reading: -3   -2   -1   0   +1   +2   +3
                                        (Circle your answer)

I can move my meter reading higher, or keep it up by:

_____

_____

_____

_____

My Gratitude Statement:

_____

_____

_____

_____

My Goal for Today:

_____

_____

_____

_____

My Action Affirmation:

_____

_____

_____

_____

Day 4

My Feeling Meter Reading: -3   -2   -1   0   +1   +2   +3

(Circle your answer)

I can move my meter reading higher, or keep it up by:

_____

_____

_____

_____

My Gratitude Statement:

_____

_____

_____

_____

My Goal for Today:

_____

_____

_____

_____

My Action Affirmation:

_____

_____

_____

_____

Day 5

My Feeling Meter Reading: -3   -2   -1   0   +1   +2   +3

(Circle your answer)

I can move my meter reading higher, or keep it up by:

_____

_____

_____

_____

My Gratitude Statement:

_____

_____

_____

_____

My Goal for Today:

_____

_____

_____

_____

My Action Affirmation:

_____

_____

_____

_____

Day 6

My Feeling Meter Reading: -3   -2   -1   0   +1   +2   +3

(Circle your answer)

I can move my meter reading higher, or keep it up by:

_____

_____

_____

_____

My Gratitude Statement:

_____

_____

_____

_____

My Goal for Today:

_____

_____

_____

_____

My Action Affirmation:

_____

_____

_____

_____

Day 7

My Feeling Meter Reading: -3   -2   -1   0   +1   +2   +3

(Circle your answer)

I can move my meter reading higher, or keep it up by:

_____

_____

_____

_____

My Gratitude Statement:

_____

_____

_____

_____

My Goal for Today:

_____

_____

_____

_____

My Action Affirmation:

_____

_____

_____

Day 8

My Feeling Meter Reading: -3   -2   -1   0   +1   +2   +3

(Circle your answer)

I can move my meter reading higher, or keep it up by:

_____

_____

_____

_____

My Gratitude Statement:

_____

_____

_____

_____

My Goal for Today:

_____

_____

_____

_____

My Action Affirmation:

_____

_____

_____

_____

Day 9

My Feeling Meter Reading: -3   -2   -1   0   +1   +2   +3

(Circle your answer)

I can move my meter reading higher, or keep it up by:

_____

_____

_____

_____

My Gratitude Statement:

_____

_____

_____

_____

My Goal for Today:

_____

_____

_____

_____

My Action Affirmation:

_____

_____

_____

_____

Day 10

My Feeling Meter Reading: -3   -2   -1   0   +1   +2   +3
(Circle your answer)

I can move my meter reading higher, or keep it up by:

_____

_____

_____

_____

My Gratitude Statement:

_____

_____

_____

_____

My Goal for Today:

_____

_____

_____

_____

My Action Affirmation:

_____

_____

_____

_____

Day 11

My Feeling Meter Reading: -3   -2   -1   0   +1   +2   +3
(Circle your answer)

I can move my meter reading higher, or keep it up by:

_____

_____

_____

_____

My Gratitude Statement:

_____

_____

_____

_____

My Goal for Today:

_____

_____

_____

_____

My Action Affirmation:

_____

_____

_____

_____

Day 12

My Feeling Meter Reading: -3   -2   -1   0   +1   +2   +3

(Circle your answer)

I can move my meter reading higher, or keep it up by:

_____

_____

_____

_____

My Gratitude Statement:

_____

_____

_____

_____

My Goal for Today:

_____

_____

_____

_____

My Action Affirmation:

_____

_____

_____

_____

Day 13

My Feeling Meter Reading: -3   -2   -1   0   +1   +2   +3
                                              (Circle your answer)

I can move my meter reading higher, or keep it up by:

_____

_____

_____

_____

My Gratitude Statement:

_____

_____

_____

_____

My Goal for Today:

_____

_____

_____

_____

My Action Affirmation:

_____

_____

_____

_____

Day 14

My Feeling Meter Reading: -3   -2   -1   0   +1   +2   +3
(Circle your answer)

I can move my meter reading higher, or keep it up by:

_____

_____

_____

_____

My Gratitude Statement:

_____

_____

_____

_____

My Goal for Today:

_____

_____

_____

_____

My Action Affirmation:

_____

_____

_____

_____

Day 15

My Feeling Meter Reading: -3   -2   -1   0   +1   +2   +3

(Circle your answer)

I can move my meter reading higher, or keep it up by:

_____

_____

_____

_____

My Gratitude Statement:

_____

_____

_____

_____

My Goal for Today:

_____

_____

_____

_____

My Action Affirmation:

_____

_____

_____

_____

Day 16

My Feeling Meter Reading: -3   -2   -1   0   +1   +2   +3

(Circle your answer)

I can move my meter reading higher, or keep it up by:

_____

_____

_____

_____

My Gratitude Statement:

_____

_____

_____

_____

My Goal for Today:

_____

_____

_____

_____

My Action Affirmation:

_____

_____

_____

_____

Day 17

My Feeling Meter Reading: -3   -2   -1   0   +1   +2   +3

(Circle your answer)

I can move my meter reading higher, or keep it up by:

_____

_____

_____

_____

My Gratitude Statement:

_____

_____

_____

_____

My Goal for Today:

_____

_____

_____

_____

My Action Affirmation:

_____

_____

_____

_____

Day 18

My Feeling Meter Reading: -3   -2   -1   0   +1   +2   +3

(Circle your answer)

I can move my meter reading higher, or keep it up by:

_____

_____

_____

_____

My Gratitude Statement:

_____

_____

_____

_____

My Goal for Today:

_____

_____

_____

_____

My Action Affirmation:

_____

_____

_____

_____

Day 19

My Feeling Meter Reading: -3   -2   -1   0   +1   +2   +3
(Circle your answer)

I can move my meter reading higher, or keep it up by:

_____

_____

_____

_____

My Gratitude Statement:

_____

_____

_____

_____

My Goal for Today:

_____

_____

_____

_____

My Action Affirmation:

_____

_____

_____

_____

Day 20

My Feeling Meter Reading: -3   -2   -1   0   +1   +2   +3
                                          (Circle your answer)

I can move my meter reading higher, or keep it up by:

_____

_____

_____

_____

My Gratitude Statement:

_____

_____

_____

_____

My Goal for Today:

_____

_____

_____

_____

My Action Affirmation:

_____

_____

_____

_____

Day 21

My Feeling Meter Reading: -3   -2   -1   0   +1   +2   +3

(Circle your answer)

I can move my meter reading higher, or keep it up by:

_____

_____

_____

_____

My Gratitude Statement:

_____

_____

_____

_____

My Goal for Today:

_____

_____

_____

_____

My Action Affirmation:

_____

_____

_____

_____

Day 22

My Feeling Meter Reading: -3   -2   -1   0   +1   +2   +3

(Circle your answer)

I can move my meter reading higher, or keep it up by:

_____

_____

_____

_____

My Gratitude Statement:

_____

_____

_____

_____

My Goal for Today:

_____

_____

_____

_____

My Action Affirmation:

_____

_____

_____

_____

Day 23

My Feeling Meter Reading: -3   -2   -1   0   +1   +2   +3

(Circle your answer)

I can move my meter reading higher, or keep it up by:

_____

_____

_____

_____

My Gratitude Statement:

_____

_____

_____

_____

My Goal for Today:

_____

_____

_____

_____

My Action Affirmation:

_____

_____

_____

_____

Day 24

My Feeling Meter Reading: -3   -2   -1   0   +1   +2   +3

(Circle your answer)

I can move my meter reading higher, or keep it up by:

_____

_____

_____

_____

My Gratitude Statement:

_____

_____

_____

_____

My Goal for Today:

_____

_____

_____

_____

My Action Affirmation:

_____

_____

_____

_____

Day 25

My Feeling Meter Reading: -3   -2   -1   0   +1   +2   +3
(Circle your answer)

I can move my meter reading higher, or keep it up by:

_____

_____

_____

_____

My Gratitude Statement:

_____

_____

_____

_____

My Goal for Today:

_____

_____

_____

_____

My Action Affirmation:

_____

_____

_____

_____

Day 26

My Feeling Meter Reading: -3   -2   -1   0   +1   +2   +3

(Circle your answer)

I can move my meter reading higher, or keep it up by:

_____

_____

_____

_____

My Gratitude Statement:

_____

_____

_____

_____

My Goal for Today:

_____

_____

_____

_____

My Action Affirmation:

_____

_____

_____

_____

Day 27

My Feeling Meter Reading: -3   -2   -1   0   +1   +2   +3
(Circle your answer)

I can move my meter reading higher, or keep it up by:

_____

_____

_____

_____

My Gratitude Statement:

_____

_____

_____

_____

My Goal for Today:

_____

_____

_____

_____

My Action Affirmation:

_____

_____

_____

_____

Day 28

My Feeling Meter Reading: -3   -2   -1   0   +1   +2   +3

(Circle your answer)

I can move my meter reading higher, or keep it up by:

_____

_____

_____

_____

My Gratitude Statement:

_____

_____

_____

_____

My Goal for Today:

_____

_____

_____

_____

My Action Affirmation:

_____

_____

_____

_____

Day 29

My Feeling Meter Reading: -3   -2   -1   0   +1   +2   +3
(Circle your answer)

I can move my meter reading higher, or keep it up by:

_____

_____

_____

_____

My Gratitude Statement:

_____

_____

_____

_____

My Goal for Today:

_____

_____

_____

_____

My Action Affirmation:

_____

_____

_____

_____

Day 30

My Feeling Meter Reading: -3   -2   -1   0   +1   +2   +3

(Circle your answer)

I can move my meter reading higher, or keep it up by:

_____

_____

_____

_____

My Gratitude Statement:

_____

_____

_____

_____

My Goal for Today:

_____

_____

_____

_____

My Action Affirmation:

_____

_____

_____

My Thank You Letter to You,

I want to thank you for doing what it takes to create a wonderful life for yourself. In doing so, you are inspiring others to do the same.

You are, right now, making our world a much better place, and you have been doing this since the day you were born.

It's your right to be happy and live your life to its absolute fullest. By taking part in this program, you are taking advantage of your right to be happy, so you deserve happiness!

I am very interested in how you are doing, and I would like to hear about some of your accomplishments and stories. Please write to me at the address below. You can also have your mom, dad, or teacher, send your story to my e-mail address.

If you ever have any questions I am always available to help you.

5025 N Central Avenue #422

Phoenix, AZ 85012

info@kidscandoanything.com

1-888-428-6470

I wish for you a wonderful life of adventure and joy, and a lifetime of happiness!

I am so grateful for you!

Patrick McMillan

Patrick McMillan
Author of "An Exercise in Happiness"

Glossary

Attracting: to pull to or toward oneself or itself
I'm thankful I am **attracting** good friends at school.

Achieve: to get by effort
You can **achieve** your dreams when you learn from your mistakes and never give up.

Believe: to accept as true
If you really think you can do something or be something that means you **believe** in yourself.

Confident: having or showing confidence
A **confident** person feels and thinks "I can do it" when they try new things.

Courageous: strength of mind to carry on, in spite of danger or difficulty
A **courageous** person is not afraid to make mistakes.

Creator: one that creates or produces
Walt Disney was the **creator** of Disneyland.

Depend: to rely for support
When we **depend** on someone, we trust and believe they will help us.

Deserve: to be worthy
All children **deserve** the right to go to school.

Eager: having or showing an impatient or enthusiastic desire or interest
He was **eager** to play in his championship baseball game today.

Encourage: to cause to feel courage, spirit, or hope
Our parents and teachers **encourage** us to do our best and be happy.

Enthusiasm: something causing a feeling of excitement and active interest
The gym was filled with **enthusiasm** by all the people that came to watch the game.

perience: skill or knowledge gained by actually doing or feeling a thing

erything that happens in your life is an **experience**.

xpert: showing special skill or knowledge gained from training or experience

expert is a person who is very experienced at something and can teach others.

naginative: of, relating to, or showing imagination

create something from your thoughts is being **imaginative**.

spiring: to cause to have a particular thought or feeling

eeing someone doing something they love doing, like singing on stage or playing a sport can

spire us to do what WE love to do.

Memory: something remembered

our **memory** is like a storage box in your mind that keeps all of your experiences.

Motivated: to provide with a reason for doing something

He was **motivated** to clean his room because as soon as he finished, his mom said he could go out

nd play.

Quote: to repeat, to give as an example

We **quote** someone if we say or write something that they said or wrote before.

Respectful: relation to or concern with something specified, marked by or showing respect

f someone is speaking, you are being **respectful** by listening.

Responsibility: being the one who must answer or account for something, the quality or state of

being responsible

He has the **responsibility** to make his bed every day before he leaves for school.

Solve: to find a solution for

Her homework for tonight includes ten math problems she needs to **solve.**

Succeed: to reach a desired end or object

I will **succeed** in school if I pay attention in class, do my homework, and study for tests.

References

Apter, Terri PhD   1997 "The Confident Child" Publisher: Bantam Trade Paperback Copyright 1997

Brodkin, Adel M. Ph.D. August10, 2006 "The Best Kept Secret about School Success" http://www2.scholastic.com/browse/article.jsp?id=7242 Parent Child Magazine

Brodkin, Adele M PhD   January 8, 2007 "You Can Do It" (Article) "So, the foremost protective factor is having a champion. Someone in their lives wit untouchable faith in their capacity to survive and succeed" http://www2.scholastic.com/browse/article.jsp?id=11275

Baumiester, Roy F., Campbell, Jennifer D., Krueger, Joachim I. Vohs, Kathleen D. MAY 2003 "Does high self-esteem cause better performance, inter-personal success, happiness or healthier life-styles" http://www.psychologicalscience.org/journals/pspi/pdf/pspi411.pdf

Carnegie, Dale 1936 How to Win Friends and Influence People: Original Copyright 1936 Renewed 1964 by Donna Dale and Dorothy Carnegie, Revise Edition Copyright 1981

Publisher: Pocket Books

Carter, Christine, PhD. 2007 UC Berkley-Institute of Human Development Blog Post "The Childhood Seeds of Adult Happiness" http://greatergood. berkeley.edu/raising_happiness/category/video/P18/ Greater Good Magazine

Clark, Lois, M.S. 2006 Ohio State University Extension, Human Development and Family Science. (Article): "Helping Children Achieve Success and Learn from Failure" Family and Consumer Sciences Ohio State University Extension,. http://fcs.osu.edu/hdfs/positiveparenting/issues.htm

Csikszentmihalyi, Mihaly 1996 Creativity; "Flow and the Psychology of Discovery and Invention" Publisher: Harper Collins, Copyright 1996.

Davis, Stan   Stop Bullying Now-Parent newsletter: http://www.stopbullyingnow.com/

Dweck, Carol, PhD April 02, 2007 Professor of Psychology Stanford University Education World E- Interview http://blog.guykawasaki.com/2007/04/ more_on_carol_d.html#axzz0wasqUAbe

Foundations for Success: Left Brain-Right Brain http://www.au.af.mil/au/awc/awcgate/army/rotc_right-left_brain.pdf

Goleman, Daniel   1995 Emotional Intelligence; "Why it can matter more than IQ" Publisher: Bantam Books Copyright1995

Gurtner, Jean-Luc, Oser, Fritz: Self-Esteem, self-concepts, personal goals and motivation – "are there age and subject differences?" University of Fribourg Switzerland, http://www.self.ox.ac.uk/Conferences/2004_Gurtner_Oser.pdf

Hicks, Jerry and Esther   "The Law of Attraction" – (The Teachings of Abraham) Copyright 2006 Publisher: Hay House

Hill, Napoleon Think and Grow Rich: Original Copyright 1937 Revised Edition "Action Manual" Copyright 1968 Revised 1972. Publisher: Penguin Group

Hallowell, Edward M, M.D 2002 The Childhood Roots of Adult Happiness "Five Steps to Help Kids Create and Sustain Lifelong Joy" Publisher: Balantine Books (Random House) Copyright 2002

Lambert, Craig Harvard Magazine Inc. (Article) 2007 – The Science of Happiness – "Psychology explores humans at their best"

Laszlo,Ervin 2007 Toward an Explanation- The Quantum Vacuum: http://www.scribd.com/doc/19348199/Ervin-Laszlo-Unus-Mundus-Subtle-Connections Grof-Jung-and-the-Quantum-Vacuum

Lybomirsky, Sonja,PhD   2007 Scientific America – (Article) The Science of Lasting Happiness: http://www.faculty.ucr.edu/~sonja/papers.html

Newitz, Annalee 11/21/2006   (Article) – "There's a scientific basis to the truism that money can't buy happiness" ALTERNET http://www.alternet.org/ tags/happiness/

Paton, Graeme 03/05/07 "Children Need Lessons in Happiness Education BBC News http://news.bbc.co.uk/2/hi/uk_news/education/6618431.stm

Reasoner, Robert   International Council for Self-Esteem: "Can the use of self-esteem programs in schools actually reduce problem behavior and create more positive school environments?" http://www.selfesteem.org/menu/aboutus/advisory/robert-reasoner.htm,

Rudin, Mike 4/30/06 BBC-The Science of Happiness (Article) http://news.bbc.co.uk/2/hi/programmes/happiness_formula/4783836.stm

Seligman, Martin E.P PhD, Reivich,, Karen Ph.D., Jaycox, Lisa Ph.D. Gilham, Jane, Ph.D.   "The Optimistic Child" Copyright 1995 Publisher: Houghton Mifflin

Seligman, Martin E.P. Ph.D. 2002 "Authentic Happiness" Copyright 2002 Publisher Simon & Shuster

Shahar, Tal Ben- Ph.D. "Happier" Author": Harvard Professor "Positive Psychology" Copyright 2007 Publisher: McGraw-Hill copyright 2007

Wallis, Claudia 2004 Time Magazine Article: The New Science of Happiness http://www.time.com/time/magazine/article/0,9171,1015902,00.html

Zins, Joseph et.al July 2007 "Building academic success on social and emotional learning"

UAMS College of Medicine- Dept. of Psychiatry's Partners in Behavior Science http://www.informaworld.com/smpp/content~db=all~content=a788024968